the
eucharist

AUTHOR:

CHIARA LUBICH was born in Trent, Italy, in 1920. She gave birth to a new spirituality in 1943 that was to become a vast movement because of the extraordinary response of people all over the world. It has attracted men and women of different denominations, married and single, laypersons, priests and religious, and especially the young. This is the Focolare Movement. Its goal is that unity for which Jesus prayed after the Last Supper, and it tries to bring about unity through the living witness of its members.

On April 7, 1977, Chiara Lubich was awarded the Templeton Foundation prize, similar to a Nobel prize, for progress in religion. She was chosen for her contributions to unity among Christians — "one of the outstanding achievements in interchurch and interfaith relations today."

Cover picture: Chiara Lubich at the Guild Hall in London about to receive the Templeton prize.

By the same author:

Stirrings of Unity (out of print)
Meditations
That All Men Be One (Origins and Life of
    the Focolare Movement)
When Our Love is Charity
A Little "Harmless" Manifesto
It's a Whole New Scene
The Word of Life
Jesus in the Midst

Cassettes:

Contemplation in the 20th Century (No. 1, 2)
God is Love
The Word of God

chiara lubich

the eucharist

new city press, new york

Published in the United States by New City Press,
the Publishing House of the Focolare Movement, Inc.
206 Skillman Avenue, Brooklyn, N.Y. 11211

© 1977 by Città Nuova Editrice, Rome, Italy
Printed in Canada
Translated from the original Italian edition *L'Eucaristia*
by the editorial staff of New City Press
Cover design by Silvio Russo

Nihil Obstat: Rev. Martin S. Rushford, Ph.D., Diocesan
Censor
Imprimatur: Francis J. Mugavero, D.D., Bishop of Brooklyn,
Brooklyn, New York, May 31, 1977
Library of Congress Catalog Number: 77-82230
ISBN 0-911782-30-3

FOREWORD

Love makes men see. Whoever loves, knows more profoundly.

Husbands and wives, parents and children, friends, and all persons who love know each other in a unique way. Outsiders are not able to understand the special rapport that exists within nuptial, paternal, and filial unions, and within all friendships.

A person who does not love lacks the light that is needed to see into the hearts of other people. But one who loves is able to discover the inner world of people around him because he does not get blocked by outward appearances.

God "who dwells in unapproachable light" (1 Tm 6:16) made himself visible in Jesus Christ. "No one has ever seen God; the only Son, who is in the bosom of the Father, he has revealed him" (Jn 1:18). In his beloved Son the Father welcomes all believers as his children, and he gives them the Spirit of his Son. Through the Spirit they are able to know God, to love him, and to call him Father (cf. Gal 4:6; Rom 8:15).

From the widsom and love of God the Father came the plan that his Son, after becoming man, would remain among men everywhere till the end of time, in order to draw all men to himself and make them perfect in unity. He is accomplishing this plan through the Eucharist, the mystery of faith, the sacrament of the true, real, and substantial presence of the risen Christ on earth.

In his parting words, Jesus quite tenderly confided to his disciples that he himself, the one who reveals the Father, would make himself known to whoever loves him: "He who loves me will be loved by my Father. I too will love him and reveal myself to him" (Jn 14:21).

What I have written so far are some thoughts that came to me while reading this book by Chiara Lubich. It is a book written with a heart full of love.

The book contains four talks Chiara Lubich gave at meetings of those responsible for the Focolare Movement throughout the world, held at Rocca di Papa (Rome) during October of 1976.

Since what she sees by faith is brought into sharper focus by love, Chiara Lubich can present profound insights into the mystery of the Eucharist. She can bring out "both the new and the old" (Mt 13:52) from the "treasure" of the Holy Scriptures and the tradition of the Church, from the riches of the Church Fathers and the theologians, and from the teachings of Vatican II and Pope Paul VI. She can penetrate the "mystery of faith" that our Savior entrusted, as a permanent remembrance of his immense love, to his spouse, the Church. Down through the centuries, the Church has preserved this sacred inheritance from the Lord and has mounted it like a jewel in precious and varied settings. And Chiara Lubich, through the particular charism she has received, is able in four short talks to make this jewel shine forth in splendor.

In the first talk, she draws upon the evidence in Holy Scripture to show us how the great plan of God for mankind is being carried out in history through the Eucharist. Through the Eucharist, Jesus Christ communicates his own immortal life to his followers so that they become one body and one blood with him.

In the second, Chiara Lubich takes us through history, and shows us how the heart of the Church has always been the Eucharist in which the beloved Son of the Father has remained among us. In addition, she makes us realize how each event that took place has "contributed in God's plan to open the eyes of the faithful to ever new aspects of the Eucharistic mystery."

In the third talk, Chiara Lubich speaks in great depth about the effects of union with the Body of Christ that has been vivified by the Holy Spirit. These effects include the divinization of man and his incorporation into Christ with his brothers. It was no suprise to hear this, since after all, it is the Ideal of the Focolare Movement. And whoever is called to live a life of unity, loves the Eucharist most fervently.

Chiara Lubich stresses in the fourth talk the firm decision of bringing about unity so that all the extraordinary graces that are contained in the Eucharist may bring forth their effect. At this point, theology and the Eucharistic spirituality of today converge with the Ideal of the Focolare Movement. Their common aim is to be one community where people live united in Christ. Divine energies flow into the community through the Eucharist. Namely, the unifying powers of faith and love, which lead all to become "one body and one spirit in Christ" (cf. Third Eucharistic prayer).

In her closing prayer, Chiara expressed her desire of "building a cathedral" for the Eucharist. Something like this has really happened, as I have been able to experience personally at a recent meeting of the Focolare in February, 1977. Her words on the Eucharist have brought to all those who have listened to them a deep understanding of this "mystery of faith" and have enkindled in them a new love for Jesus in the Eucharist. And the Eucharist transformed their hearts, making of

10

many one and building them all into a kind of cathedral through the Holy Spirit.

May this book find many readers who will see Jesus in the Eucharist with faith, love him in unity, and glorify him by giving thanks.

† Josef Stimpfle
Bishop of Augsburg

Augsburg, May 17, 1977

CONTENTS

13

The Eucharist and the New Testament

For me to talk about you, Jesus in the Eucharist, is really quite daring and presumptuous. For you are present in all the churches of the world, listening to the intimate secrets, the hidden problems, and the sighs of millions of people, seeing the tears of joy in the conversions you alone know about. You are the heart of all hearts, the heart of the Church.

We would prefer not to disturb the silence which is fitting for such a sublime and breathtaking love, except that our own love, eager to overcome every fear, desires to get beyond the veils of the white host and the wine in the golden chalice.

Forgive our daring: for love wants to know better in order to love better. We do not want our journey on earth to be over before we have discovered at least a little about who you are.

Also, since we are Christians, and within our mother the Church we live and spread the Ideal of unity, we have to talk about the Eucharist, for none of the mysteries of our faith has so much to do with unity as the Eucharist. The Eucharist opens up unity and reveals its substance. In fact, it is through the Eucharist that man's unity with God is completely fulfilled, as well as the unity among men and the unity of the whole cosmos with its Creator.

God became man. And Jesus came on earth. It was in his power to do everything and anything. But the logic of love demanded that once he had taken a step like this, that is, to come from the Trinity down to life on earth, he would not stay here for only thirty-three years, although his life on earth was divinely extraordinary. Rather, he had to find a way to remain, and make himself present in every corner of the earth throughout the centuries, and to remain in the culminating moment of his love, the moment of his sacrifice and glory, his death and resurrection. He has remained here. For with divine imagination, he invented the Eucharist. This shows his love reaching beyond all possible limits. *St. Therese of Lisieux* put it this way: "O Jesus, permit me to say, brimming over with gratitude, that your love goes so far as to become madness."[1]

Institution of the Eucharist

Let's see how the event is related by *Matthew, Mark, Luke* and *Paul. Luke* says: "When the hour arrived, he took his place at table, and the apostles with him. He said to them: 'I have greatly desired to eat this Passover with you before I suffer. I tell you, I will not eat again until it is fulfilled in the kingdom of God.' . . . Then, taking bread and giving thanks, he broke it and gave it to them, saying: 'This is my body to be given for you; Do this as a remembrance of me.' He did the same with the cup after eating, saying as he did so: 'This cup is the new covenant in my blood, which will be shed for you'." (Lk 22: 14-20). It is only because he is God, that Jesus could unveil realities which were so new, so unforeseeable, so infathomable, using so few solemn words. These realities could send us into ecstasy because, if we understood them even a little, our human nature could not stand up in front of them.

Jesus was the only one who knew everything, the only one who was aware that his gesture was bringing centuries of expectation to an end, the only one who could look into the infinite consequences of what he was, i.e., the fulfillment of a divine plan which had always been foreseen by the Trinity, the foundation of the Church. It is a plan which starts on earth but penetrates into the mysteries of the Kingdom. Only God could have spoken and behaved in that way.

However, something of what his most Sacred Heart felt in that moment shines through those words "I have greatly desired." They express an immense joy. And the words "Before I suffer" express his embrace of the Cross and the bond between suffering and joy, because he was about to make his last will and testament, and a will is not valid until after death. He was leaving us an immense inheritance: himself.

St. Peter Julian Eymard says: "Jesus Christ too wants to leave his own memorial, his own masterpiece, which would render him immortal in the hearts of his people. It will be an undying reminder of his love for man. He will be its inventor, its author. He will consecrate it as his testament. And his death will give it life and glory. . . . This is the divine Eucharist."[2]

Then Jesus "gave thanks." Eucharist means "great thanksgiving" and the most perfect thanksgiving was the one Jesus made to the Father for having watched over mankind and having saved it by intervening in the most extraordinary ways.

Then taking the bread and the cup he said: "This is my body to be given for you. Do this as a remembrance of me. . . . This cup is the new covenant in my blood which will be shed for you."

This is the Eucharist. It is the great miracle. The Eucharist, in *St. Thomas Aquinas'* words, is the greatest of the miracles of Jesus Christ.[3] In fact, as *Peter Julian Eymard* said, "It is superior to all the others in its object and surpasses all the others in its duration. It is Jesus' permanent incarnation and perpetual sacrifice. It's like the burning bush burning on the altar forever. It is the manna, the true bread of life which comes down daily from heaven."[4]

These are, to use *Ignatius of Antioch's* expression, "mysteries, loudly proclaimed tó the world though accomplished in the stillness of God!"[5] And the *Second Vatican Council* affirms that, "the Most Blessed Eucharist contains the Church's entire spiritual wealth, that is, Christ Himself, our Passover and living bread. Through his very flesh, made vital and vitalizing by the Holy Spirit, He offers life to men."[6]

From the Old to the New Testament

Jesus celebrates his Passover as a banquet. In every home, suppertime is the time of the deepest intimacy, brotherhood, and often of friendship and of celebration.

The banquet over which Jesus presides is celebrated as the Passover of the Jews, and as such it contains in synthesis the entire history of the people of Israel. The last supper of Jesus is the fulfillment of all God's promises. The "elements" of the new supper are pregnant with meaning acquired in the Old Testament. Bread was considered a gift of God, indispensable to life; it was a symbol of communion, a reminder of the manna. Wine, called in *Genesis* the "blood of grapes" (49:11), was offered in sacrifices (Ex 29:40). It was a symbol of the joy of the future messianic times (cf. Jer 31:12). The cup was a sign of participation in that joy and acceptance of afflictions. It was a reminder of the Covenant of Moses (cf. Ex 24:6). Both bread and wine had been promised by Wisdom to her disciples (cf. Prv 9:1-6).[7]

Like the father of a family, Jesus, in his gestures and in the prayer of benediction, repeats the Judaic rite. But this banquet is totally different and new if compared with the Hebrew Passover: the supper of Jesus is celebrated in the context of his passion and death. In the Eucharist he anticipates, in a symbolic and real way, his redemptive sacrifice. He is both the priest and the victim.

20

Pope Paul VI expressed himself in this way on Holy Thursday of 1966: "We cannot forget that his supper . . . was a commemorative rite; it was the paschal meal which had to be repeated every year in order to transmit to future generations the indelible reminder of the Hebrew people's liberation from slavery in Egypt. . . . This evening Jesus substitutes the new covenant for the old. "This is my blood", he will say, "of the New Covenant" (Mt 26:28). With these words Jesus joins his own Passover to the ancient, historical, and figurative Passover and makes it succeed it. Jesus' Passover is also historical, but it is final, and at the same time an image of another final event: the Parousia [the Second Coming of Jesus]."[8]

The words "I will not drink this fruit of the vine from now until the day when I drink it new with you in my Father's reign" (Mt 26:29) — the last phrase was translated by a famous Scripture scholar as "an appointment in Paradise"[9] — give the Eucharist the character of a banquet which will find its completion after our Resurrection. In reference to the New Testament passover, *St. Athanasius* writes: "Already here on earth we can participate in the communion with the risen Christ. . . . We participate, my beloved, not in a temporary feast but in that which is eternal and heavenly, and we do not portray it with images but we realize it in truth." Indeed, we no longer eat the flesh of a lamb but "we eat the Word of the Father." 'For *Athanasius,* to eat the bread and wine changed into the body and blood of Christ is to celebrate the passover, that is, to relive it. The Eucharist is indeed a sacrament of communion with the paschal Christ, with a Christ who died and is risen, who has passed over (pasch = passage). He entered into a new phase of his existence, the glorious one at the right hand of the Father. Therefore, receiving Jesus in the Eucharist really means participating — already here on earth — in his life of glory, in his communion with the Father.[10]

The Bread of Life

John has his own way of speaking about Jesus in the Eucharist. In the sixth chapter of his Gospel, he tells us that Jesus, the day after multiplying the loaves, gave a great discourse in Capernaum which included these words: "You should not be working for perishable food but for food that remains until life eternal, food which the Son of Man will give you" (Jn 6:27). A little later Jesus presents himself as the true bread that came down from heaven, which is to be received in faith. "I myself am the bread of life. No one who comes to me shall ever

22

be hungry. No one who believes in me shall ever thirst" (Jn 6:35).

And he explains how he will be the bread of life: ". . .the bread I will give is my flesh for the life of the world. . ." (Jn 6:51 b).

Jesus already sees himself as bread. That, therefore, is the ultimate purpose of his life here on earth: to be bread in order to be eaten, and to be eaten in order to communicate his own life to us.

"This is the bread that comes down from heaven for a man to eat and never die. I myself am the Living Bread come down from heaven. If anyone eats this bread he shall live forever" (Jn 6:50-51a).

How limited are our views compared with those of Jesus. He, who is infinite, who comes from eternity, has protected a people with miracles and graces. He has built his church, and sets it on its way towards eternity where life will never end.

During this brief existence of ours, we are often shortsighted and at times we worry over trifles. We are blind; yes, blind. We Christians too are often blind. We may live our faith, but without being fully conscious of it. We understand Jesus in some of his words, which give us consolation or some direction, but we do not see the whole Jesus.

"In the beginning was the Word," then came creation, then the incarnation. And then, by means of the Holy Spirit, we have almost a second incarnation in the Eucharist, which serves us as food in this life while on our journey towards the next. Finally, once we are made divine by his person present in his body and blood in the Eucharist, we will reach the Kingdom with Jesus.

When we look at reality in this way, everything acquires its true value. Everything is directed towards the future that we shall reach if we try to live the life of the heavenly city even here below as much as possible. We live it if we are careful, in loving God and all of mankind, to have a love similar to Jesus' love. What an adventure is life!

The pharisees argued with one another, and Jesus replied and explained, and then reaffirmed his words by saying, "He who feeds on my flesh and drinks my blood remains in me and I in him. Just as the Father who has life sent me, and I have life because of the Father, so the man who feeds on me will have life because of me" (Jn 6:56-67).

"He remains in me and I in him." This shows the unity established between Jesus and the human person who feeds on him made bread. What is transmitted to men is the fullness of life that is in Jesus and comes to him from the Father. In this way, a man becomes immanent in Jesus.

Albert the Great writes, Christ "embraced us with too much love, because he united us to himself so closely that he is within us, and he himself penetrates into our innermost parts. . . .

"Divine love produces an ecstasy. It is right to say this of divine love because it brings God into us and us into God. The Greek term *ekstasis,* in fact, means 'being outside oneself.' [Jesus] says, indeed, 'The man who feeds on my flesh and drinks my blood remains in me and I in him' (Jn 6:56). He says, 'He remains in me,' that is, he dwells outside of himself; and 'I remain in him,' that is, I dwell outside of myself. . . . This can be done by his charity, which penetrates into us . . . and attracts us to him. . . . It does not just attract us but it takes us into himself, and he penetrates into us to the very marrow of our bones.[11]

In this stupendous chapter of the Gospel of John, Jesus affirms, "The bread I will give is my flesh for the life of the world" (6:51d). And again, "He who feeds on my flesh and drinks my blood has life eternal and I will raise him up on the last day" (6:54).

"For the life of the world." The Eucharist, therefore, serves even in this world for giving us life. But what is life? Jesus told us: "I am the life" (Jn 11:25;14:6). This bread nourishes us on him already here below.

"And I will raise him up on the last day." But what is the Resurrection? Jesus told us: "I am the Resurrection" (Jn 11:25). The Eucharist also gives us life for the other world.

He starts in us his own immortal life, that life which is not interrupted by death. Even though our bodies are corruptible, Christ, the life, remains in our souls and in our bodies as the principle of our immortality.

The resurrection is simply a great mystery for all those who approach it with human reason alone. But there is a way of living which makes the mystery less incomprehensible. When one lives the Gospel seen from the perspective of unity, he experiences, for example, that in carrying out the new commandment of Jesus, mutual love leads to a fraternal unity among people that goes beyond natural, human love. This result, this achievement, is an effect of doing God's will. Jesus in fact knew that if we responded to his immense gifts, we would no longer be his servants or friends but his brothers, and brothers with one another, because we would all be nourished on the same life, his life.

To indicate this different kind of family, *John* the evangelist uses an evocative image: the vine and the branches (15). The same sap, or we could say the same blood, the same life, that is, the same love (which is the love with which the Father loves the Son) is communicated to us (17:23-26) and circulates between Jesus and us. We become, therefore, one blood and one body with Christ. It is, then, in the truest and supernaturally deepest sense of the word that Jesus after his resurrection calls his disciples "brothers" (Jn 20:17). The author of the Epistle to the Hebrews confirms that the risen Jesus "is not ashamed to call them brothers" (Heb 2:11).

Now, once this family of the kingdom of heaven had been formed, how could anyone conceive of death putting an end to such a work of a God? No, God could not involve us in such an absurdity and leave us there. He had to give us a solution, and he gave it by revealing the truth of the resurrection of the flesh. This truth turns out to be no longer a dark mystery of faith for the

27

believer, but a logical consequence of Christian living. It gives us the immense joy of knowing that we will all meet again with Jesus who has united us as brothers.

The Eucharist in the Acts of the Apostles

In divine revelation we find the Eucharist again mentioned in the *Acts of the Apostles*. The early Church was very faithful to Jesus in fulfilling the "Do this in remembrance of me." Of the first community in Jerusalem it is said that "They devoted themselves to the apostles' instruction and the communal life, to the breaking of bread and the prayers" (Acts 2:42). And we read about Paul's apostolate: "On the first day of the week when we gathered for the breaking of bread, Paul preached to them. Because he intended to leave the next day, he kept on speaking until midnight. . . . Afterward Paul . . . broke bread, and ate. Then he talked for a long while — until his departure at dawn" (Acts 20:7, 11).

The Eucharist in the Letters of Paul

Also, in his First Letter to the Corinthians, *Paul* showed how ardent and firm was his faith in the Body and Blood of Christ, by writing: "Is not the cup of blessing we bless a sharing in the blood of Christ? And

28

is not the bread we break a sharing in the body of Christ?" And he continues by describing the effect that this mysterious bread works in the persons who receive it: "Because the loaf of bread is one we, many though we are, are one body, for we all partake of the one loaf" (1 Cor 10:16-17).

One body! This is the commentary of *St. John Chrysostom:* "We are that selfsame body. For what is the bread? The Body of Christ. And what do they become who partake of it? The body of Christ: not many bodies, but one body. For as the bread consisting of many grains is made one, so that the grains nowhere appear, so are we conjoined both with each other and with Christ."[12]

Jesus, you have a great plan for us, and you are fulfilling it in the course of the centuries. You want to make us one with you so that we may be where you are. After you came from the Trinity down to earth, it was the will of the Father that you return. However, you did not want to return alone, but together with us. This, then, is the long journey: from the Trinity back to the Trinity, passing through the mysteries of life and death, of suffering and glory.

Fortunately, the Eucharist is also a thanksgiving. Only through the Eucharist can we ever thank you enough.

29

The Celebration of the Eucharist in the Life of the Church

The history of how the Eucharist has been understood down through the centuries, is marked by a deepening awareness of it as, above all others, "the mystery of our faith."

Everything has contributed to unveil the infinite wealth which it contains. Every happy or sad occurence, the Ecumenical Councils, the ever-watchful and infallible magisterium of the Church, the vital experiences of the saints, the heresies, the wars, the bitter negations, all contributed in God's plan to open the eyes of the faithful to ever new aspects of the Eucharistic mystery. As *St. Catherine of Siena* says, it is "all God and all man.''

God the Son, in his immense love, wished to remain among us. God the Father made all things come

together so that Christians would always better understand the Eucharist and what it does for each individual
and all humanity. Like the sun which gradually
increases the effects of its heat and light until midday,
so the understanding of the Eucharist has grown
throughout the centuries.

This is no place to dwell on particular historical
events, but I will say something in order to praise God.
Furthermore, everything concerning the one we love is
of immense interest to us.

The Celebration of the Eucharist in the Early Church

As long as the Church has existed, the Eucharist
has always been its heart. We can see that the life of the
first generations of the Church revolved around the
celebration of the Eucharist. All of its doctrinal and vital
aspects were brought into light in the writings of the
apostolic fathers and of the apologists, as well as in the
Acts of the Martyrs.

In the year 155 *Justin Martyr* described the liturgical
celebration as follows: "On the day which is called Sunday we have a common assembly of all who live in the

cities or in the outlying districts, and the memoirs of the Apostles or the writings of the Prophets are read, as long as there is time. Then, when the reader has finished, the president of the assembly verbally admonishes and invites all to imitate such examples of virtue. Then we all stand up together and offer up our prayers. . . . At the conclusion of the prayers we greet one another with a kiss. Then, bread and a chalice containing wine mixed with water are presented to the one presiding over the brethren. He takes them and offers praise and glory to the Father of all through the name of the Son and of the Holy Spirit, and he recites lengthy prayers and thanksgiving to God in the name of those to whom he granted such favors. At the end of these prayers and thanksgiving, all present express their approval by saying 'Amen.' . . . And when he who presides has celebrated the Eucharist, they whom we call deacons permit each one present to partake of the Eucharistic bread, and wine and water; and they carry it also to the absentees."[13]

And a little further on we find already in *Justin* an expression of exceptional importance regarding the real presence: "The food which has been made Eucharist by the prayer of his word . . . is both the flesh and blood of that Jesus who was made flesh."[14]

33

Furthermore, *Justin* maintained that objectively the Eucharist is a sacrifice, stressing however that it is a sacrifice of an altogether new type. There is no place any longer for the bloody material sacrifices of the Old Testament. The Eucharist represents the long-awaited spiritual sacrifice since the Word himself is the victim.

The Eucharist also reinforces fraternal charity. Immediately after the distribution of the consecrated elements, wrote Justin, "the wealthy, if they wish, contribute whatever they desire, and the collection is placed in the custody of the president. [With it] he helps the orphans and widows, those who are needy because of sickness or any other reason, and the captives and strangers in our midst; in short, he takes care of all those in need."[15] It was already said in the *Didache* that the Eucharistic bread is a symbol of the unity among the brothers who form the church: "As this broken bread was scattered upon the mountain tops and after being harvested was made one, so let thy Church be gathered together from the ends of the earth into thy kingdom."[16]

Ignatius of Antioch around the year 100 described the Christian community gathered around the bishop and already structured. "Let all follow the bishop as Jesus Christ did the Father, and the priests, as you

34

would the Apostles. Reverence the deacons as you would the command of God. Apart from the bishop, let no one perform any of the functions that pertain to the Church. Let that Eucharist be held valid which is offered by the bishop or by one to whom the bishop has committed this charge."[17]

A number of martyrs from the first apostolic communities associated their own sacrifice with the Eucharist. When he was bound to the stake for example, *St. Polycarp of Smyrna* prayed as follows: "God . . . of the whole creation . . . I bless thee, for having made me worthy of this day and hour; I bless thee, because I may have a part along with the martyrs, in the chalice of thy Christ, unto resurrection in eternal life, resurrection both of soul and body in the incorruptibility of the Holy Spirit."[18]

Irenaeus, maintaining that God became a man in order that we might become children of God, considered the Eucharist the cause of the resurrection of the flesh: "also our bodies, when they receive the Eucharist, are no longer corruptible, having the hope of the resurrection to eternity."[19]

These passages have great value. For the most part they come from the very disciples of the apostles. The chief points we find in them are: Christ as the center of the community in the celebration of the Eucharist; real communion with the body and the blood of Christ; the Eucharist as a sacrifice; the Christians' awareness of forming one single body through the Eucharist; the sharing of material goods; the crucial importance of unity with the bishop; the bond between one's own sacrifice and that of the Eucharist; and the Eucharist as the cause of our resurrection.

We note also that the liturgical celebration took place in general on "the Lord's day" as a memorial of Christ's resurrection, and that it was presented at once as a sacred rite even if it preserved a family character. It already followed a definite pattern, though not rigid, made up of readings, prayers, the offering and consecration of the bread and of the wine mixed with water, and then communion for those present and for absentees.

This format will stay unchanged until the peace of Constantine (313 A.D.) but with a tendency to give an always greater emphasis to the rite itself.

The Golden Age of the Liturgy in the East and in the West [20]

Then came the golden age of the liturgy in the East and in the West, from 300 to about 900 A.D. The Fathers of the Church studied the celebration of the Eucharist from various aspects, especially as the presentation of the passion, death, and resurrection of Jesus. They explained how the faithful should participate in it, namely, by the offering of their own beings and by living their lives in charity.

This period saw the birth of the great liturgical communities around the patriarchal sees. The celebration no longer had the domestic and homelike appearance of a supper, but turned into a solemn ceremony which went together with a clearer understanding of the grandeur of the rite.

Deep theological maturity and spiritual riches were expressed in the "Eucharistic prayers" (or canons) which become fixed and obligatory. Even if they were said by the bishop or by a priest appointed by him, they were always an expression of the entire ecclesial community. This was the reason for the use of the plural "we."

The Eucharistic prayers, even in their variety, remained constant in some essential features: (a) thanksgiving and praise to the Father for having sent Christ to accomplish the salvation of mankind; (b) invocation of the Father, that he send the Holy Spirit to consecrate the bread and the wine and then to sanctify those participating; (c) commemoration of the Last Supper, which renews each time Christ's sacrifice, to which the entire Church unites its own sacrifice; and (d) remembrance of the saints in heaven, expressing the communion with the whole Church, and asking their intercession for the whole world.

The instructions following the Second Vatican Council have added to the Roman Canon, three other Eucharistic prayers taken from the liturgy of this golden age. We will use as an example the second Eucharistic prayer, which developed from the anaphora of Hippolytus (230 A.D.) and is called "the Canon of the Age of the Martyrs."[21] We find in it part (a) devoted to thanksgiving and praise to the Father:

> Father, it is our duty and our salvation . . .
> to give you thanks
> through your beloved son Jesus Christ.
> He is . . . the Savior you sent to redeem us.
> [Through this mystery of salvation]

we join the angels and saints
in proclaiming your glory
as we sing (say):
Holy, holy, holy Lord. . . .

(b) We come to the invocation of the Father that he send the Holy Spirit:

Let your Spirit come upon these gifts to make them holy,
So that they may become for us
the body and blood of our Lord, Jesus Christ.

And later this is added:

May all of us who share in the body and blood of Christ
be brought together in unity by the Holy Spirit.

(c) There is the commemoration of the Last Supper:

. . . he took bread and gave you thanks.
He broke the bread,
gave it to his disciples, and said:
Take this all of you and eat it:
This is my body which will be given up for you.
. . . Do this in memory of me.

(d) Finally, we see expressed the communion of the whole Church on earth and in heaven:

Lord, remember your Church throughout the
    world;
make us grow in love,
together with . . . our Pope . . .
Remember our brothers and sisters
who have gone to their rest
in the hope of rising again . . .
Have mercy on us all;
make us worthy to share eternal life
with Mary the Virgin Mother of God,
with the apostles,
and with all the saints . . .

The Eucharist in the West during the Middle Ages

The fundamental format of the Mass had been
defined and solidified. Now it was necessary to bring out
another aspect of the Eucharist: the real presence of
Jesus and his personal relationship with each of us.
God's providence makes use of everything to manifest
the truth.

In the Eucharist Jesus is not understood any better
than when he was on earth.

The great schism of the Eastern Church and the
political developments of the time had an influence on

40

the liturgy, for it lost much of its popular and communitarian character. The Eucharistic prayer was recited in such a way that the faithful could hardly hear it. Communion was given under only one species. Private Masses multiplied. The faithful began to desert communion. The figure of the priest became too prominent. For some allegorists the celebration of the Mass became nothing more than a representation of the passion and death of the Lord with strangely dramatic ceremonies and gestures. The liturgical crisis was accompanied by the dogmatic one which went so far as to deny the presence of Christ in the Eucharist.

But then came the triumph of the Holy Spirit, who makes all things work together for the good of the Church. The Church showed a reaction through its faith in the real presence of Christ in the Eucharist. This gave birth to the ritual worship of the Eurcharist in itself. The feast of Corpus Christi was introduced with benedictions, expositions and processions of the Blessed Sacrament.

People found in the adoration of the Blessed Sacrament, the most meaningful way of celebrating the Eucharist. *Thomas Aquinas* became the theologian and the singer of the personal presence of Christ, true God and true man, in the Eucharist.

From the Council of Trent to the Current Liturgical Renewal

The year 1500 brought in the era of the Protestant Reformation which repudiated the adoration of the Eucharist and the sacrifice of the Mass. At the same time, through the *Council of Trent* the Holy Spirit strongly affirmed the truth of the real presence and of the sacrifice of Christ in the Mass. On the real presence, the Council of Trent taught the following: " 'after the consecration of the bread and wine, our Lord Jesus Christ, true God and true Man, is really, truly, and substantially contained under those outward appearances.' In this way, the Savior in his humanity is present not only at the right hand of the Father according to the natural manner of existence, but also in the sacrament of the Eucharist 'by a mode of existence which we cannot express in words, but which, with a mind illumined by faith, we can conceive, and must most firmly believe, to be possible to God.' "[22]

Regarding the Mass as the sacrifice of Christ, the Council affirmed that "through the mystery of the Eucharist, the sacrifice of the cross, which was once offered on Calvary, is remarkably re-enacted and constantly recalled, and its saving power exerted for the forgiveness of those sins we daily commit."[23]

42

In the last four centuries the importance given to the adoration of the Blessed Sacrament and communion was an indication of the greater understanding of the Eucharistic mystery. Even communion was considered more as worship of Christ who is present, than as participation in the Eucharistic banquet. There followed different manifestations of this worship of Jesus in the Eucharist: Forty Hours devotions, visits to the Blessed Sacrament, Eucharistic Congresses. Congregations and religious institutes whose members were dedicated to the adoration of the Blessed Sacrament, were founded. Included among them are the Blessed Sacrament Fathers and the spiritual families of Charles de Foucauld.

This was a time in which the truths of the faith and the commitment to the Christian life were kept alive to such an extent as to create masterpieces of sanctity in many persons.

The Eucharist in Our Age

Then came our own age. Without losing an appreciation of what the people understand, the Church, which comprehends the whole and gives the right value to everything, used its teaching authority to bring back into balance aspects of the liturgy which had lost clarity and popularity. All this was done without ignoring what the majority of people had already understood.

The invitations of Pope Pius X to frequent communion and to communion for children were the prelude of a new era. The liturgical renewal, which developed first in Belgium and then in Germany, lead to a rediscovery of the theological and pastoral values of the Eucharist. This renewal drew from the sources of primitive liturgy, the writings of the Fathers of the Church, and from Scripture.

At the same time, the persecutions suffered by Christians in Germany which compelled them to live a catacomb life, prompted them to relive with joy the primitive Eucharistic liturgies.

Pius XII in his encyclical *Mediator Dei* (1947) reconciled what was old and new in the Church and especially with regard to the Eucharistic liturgy. In the last few years with the Second Vatican Council and the encyclical *Mysterium Fidei* of *Paul VI* (1965), all aspects of the celebration of the Mass have been brought back into the light: the Eucharist as a memorial, as the sacrifice of Jesus and of the Church, and as a banquet of communion with Christ and with our brothers. The Mass has acquired simpler and more homelike forms with a greater participation by the people. It has reflected the commitment to charity and to communion which fits in with modern needs particularly well.

The *Second Vatican Council* says: "At the last Supper, on the night when he was betrayed, Our Savior instituted the Eucharistic Sacrifice of his Body and Blood. He did this in order to perpetuate the sacrifice of the Cross throughout the centuries until He should come again, and so to entrust to his beloved spouse, the Church, a memorial of his death and resurrection: a sacrament of love, a sign of unity, a bond of charity, a paschal banquet in which Christ is consumed, the mind is filled with grace, and a pledge of future glory is given to us.

"The Church therefore earnestly desires that Christ's faithful, when present at this mystery of faith, should not be there as strangers or silent spectators. On the contrary, through a proper appreciation of the rites and prayers they should participate knowingly, devoutly, and actively. They should be instructed by God's word and be refreshed at the table of the Lord's body; they should give thanks to God by offering the Immaculate Victim, not only through the hands of the priest but also together with him, they should learn to offer themselves too. Through Christ the mediator, they should be drawn day by day into ever closer union with God and with each other, so that finally God may be all in all."[24]

Reading these passages on the liturgy of our times, I found the answer to a question I had often asked myself: What characterizes or is special about the Focolarini who have become priests after living for years a life of total sharing of possessions and of mutual love with the members of their community? And the answer was difficult because what they have is too simple. Now I am beginning to understand: they are the priests the Church wants today. Love has led them to break down every barrier between them and their brothers. Therefore they celebrate Mass either in the Focolare community where they live or on the occasion of large gatherings (Conventions, Mariapolises) of thousands of persons. The people attending are already united with them in the name of Jesus, as they ought to be.

In fact, the introduction to the new Sunday missal says, "From the first moment of their meeting, Christians who come from different places and environments ought to recognize each other as brothers. Their unity is created by Christ present in their midst. He indeed has said: "Where two or three are gathered in my name there am I in their midst.' (Mt 18:20)"[25]

The rite of a Mass celebrated in a Focolare community is simple and homelike. The Mass involves everyone and not only the priest. Those who are readers prepare themselves well. Songs are carefully selected; for instance, the entrance song expresses the joy of the assembling community. People spontaneously express their intentions at the prayer of the faithful. And the priest is there at the center to renew in Christ's name the sacrifice of the Cross.

The presence of Jesus among the participants touches the hearts of the people, who arrive at the most difficult decisions as if they were alone with Jesus present on the altar. Once a child told me: "During Mass I felt as if I were with Jesus alone." This means that the community was one soul with the priest and with Christ on the altar and nothing disturbed that unity. Mass is the center and the high point of our meetings. Everything is a preparation for this personal encounter with Christ, and almost all the participants receive the Eucharist. After this, the assembly is filled with joy which bears witness to their unity with the risen Christ.

At the end of Mass, the priest and faithful leave as though in a continuation of the Mass itself. They go in order to bring charity into their homes, offices, factories — all their environments. There, the communion continues and sets people free. They go out to encourage other human beings to go ahead, whatever the circumstances and whatever the place in the whole world; this becomes an obligation in order to love as Jesus loved.

This is the people of God which is more of God now, where the sharing of goods is silent but constant and growing and serving a thousand needs; where communion with Christ grows in the living of his word, where longing for evangelization inflames people's hearts.

These are our priests: completely united with the people of God, representatives of the people at the altar, vicars of Christ who is the head of his body, Christ himself in his holy memorial. Our priests are . . . priests. Theirs is an extraordinary adventure.

Unity with Christ and with Our Brothers

In the previous chapters we have brought together and explained a little the Scripture passages concerning the institution of the Eucharist. We have considered also the liturgical and dogmatic development of the Eucharist throughout the centuries. After all this, we might get the impression that we have said everything. But what depths are hidden in the words of God! They contain God himself.

The Eucharist Unites Us to Christ

Let us see now the difference between the union with God which the Eucharist brings about and that which is the effect of other sacraments.

Other sacraments join us to Jesus through their own power, that is, through the specific grace that each sacrament gives. For example, the sacrament of matrimony gives the grace a person needs to live in unity with Christ in married life.

In the Eucharist, however, we are united to Jesus himself substantially present, because in the Eucharist we eat his flesh and drink his blood, as John says (cf. Jn 6:53-56).

Baptism, in which water is used to signify the washing away of original sin and other sins, is the sacrament of new birth. It is something personal, and it is received only once in a lifetime.

The Eucharist is food. And food is taken every day in order to maintain and to increase life. *Thomas Aquinas* says: "This sacrament is given under the form of food and drink. Therefore every effect which is produced for physical life by material food and drink, that is sustenance, growth, regeneration and pleasure, all of these effects are produced by this sacrament for the spiritual life."[26] And again, "As physical food is necessary for life, so much so that one cannot live without it . . . so also spiritual food is necessary for the spiritual life, so much so that without it, one's spiritual life cannot be maintained."[27]

Thomas Aquinas also says that the one who does the generating (as Christ in Baptism) makes the one generated (man) into his image, but does not assimilate him into his own substance.[28]

The Eucharist, however, produces a union of the faithful with God which goes far beyond that produced by Baptism; it achieves a substantial assimilation. All of this, of course, has to be understood in such a way that we respect the distance between creator and creature. There is no physical fusion between the communicant and Christ; there is a mystical assimilation, spiritual but real, which allows one precisely to use the term *body, one body*.[29]

In the documents of *Vatican II* we read that communion with the body and blood of Christ does nothing less than change us into what we received.[30] This has been demonstrated by the great heights of mystical experience, by the transforming union, that some saints have reached precisely through communion. Because the union between Christ and his Church is so complete, it has the character of a marriage; and this deep unity is also experienced in the union between Christ and the individual soul.

Having said this, we can understand the amazing statement of *Thomas Aquinas:* "The proper effect of the Eucharist is the transformation of man into God": his divinization.[31]

When we read the works of the Fathers and the saints, we find that they reveal to us the reality of the Eucharist and its effects on persons receiving it with the proper disposition, in a very new way.

We expressed an intuition of this reality in a talk to the first international school for Focolarini in 1961. Among other things, I said then: "God became a man in order to save us. When he had become a man, however, he desired to become food so that, feeding ourselves on him, each of us might become another Jesus. Now, it is one thing to see Jesus as if we had lived in his times; it is another thing to re-live Jesus, to be able to be another Jesus upon earth today. The Eucharist has precisely this purpose: to nourish us with Jesus in order to transform us into another Jesus because he has loved us as himself."

We Christians have spoken and heard too many words with too little understanding of the love of Christ for us: "As the Father has loved me, so I have loved you" (Jn 15:9). That word "as" is really true. That is how we are loved. And so we can be other Christs, by means of the Eucharist. Do we realize it? If we realized it, by now the world would have been changed.

Jesus in the Eucharist, give me the grace, as I read the Fathers of your Church and your saints, to make you a little better known. This is the longing I feel in these days, I am almost distressed at my inadequacy, at my inability to express what you have given me to experience when close to you. It is too great. May the Holy Spirit make up for what I am unable to do. Or, better yet, may he take over completely. He has a lot to do with the Eucharist.

The Holy Spirit can shed light upon the words of the Fathers and of the saints. He can move our hearts and open our eyes so that we can see our destiny and the indescribable love of Jesus for us.

Here is what we discovered in *Cyril of Jerusalem:* "In the figure of bread his body is given to you, and in the figure of wine his blood, that by partaking of the body and blood of Christ you may become one body and one blood with him."

We can speak of one body and blood not because a physical union is brought about, but because of the union of our persons with the glorified body of Christ, which is present in the Eucharist and is vivified by the Holy Spirit. We are, therefore, really one body, but in a new and mystical sense.

Cyril continues, "For when his body and blood become absorbed into the members of our bodies, we become Christ-bearers, so that, as *St. Peter* said, we become 'sharers of the divine nature' (2Pt. 1:4)."[32]

And *Leo the Great:* "For nothing else is brought about by the partaking of the body and blood of Christ than that we become what we eat; and both in spirit and in body we carry about everywhere Christ in whom and with whom we were dead, buried, and rose again."[33]

Augustine too writes as if he had heard a voice from on high: "I am the food of grown men: grow great and you shall eat of me. And you shall not change me into yourself as bodily food, but you shall be changed into me."[34]

And Doctor of the Church *Albert the Great* writes in several different works: "This sacrament changes us into the body of Christ, in order that we may be bone of his bones, flesh of his flesh, and members of his members."[35]

"Every time two things are united in such a way that one has to be changed into all of the other, then the stronger transforms into itself that which is weaker. Therefore, since this food possesses greater power than those who eat of it, this food transforms into itself those who eat it."[36]

"Those who have received him [Jn 1:12] in the sacrament, eating him spiritually, become of one body with his Son, and so they are and they are called sons of God."

"In this generation the Lord's Body is like a seed which uses its power to attract man to itself and transform him into itself."

"How much we must thank Christ who with his life-giving Body changes us into himself in order that we may become his holy body pure and divine."[37]

Next we will mention the writings of a few saints. Taking them by themselves they might perhaps seem exaggerated, sentimental, even insane. But the Fathers confirm their words and confirm that they are saints.

St. Therese of Lisieux tells how she met with Jesus: "That day it was no longer a *glance* but a *fusion*. There were no longer *two*. Therese had vanished like a drop of water in the ocean. Only Jesus remained. He was the master, he the king."[38] This experience ought not to be an isolated case reserved for exceptional souls. It ought to be and to become more of a common experience for all Christians if they receive communion with all the necessary conditions we will mention in the next chapter.

We have persons in the Movement who are witnesses to this because they have lived intensely all that was required for the Eucharist to produce its full effect. God made them understand that they had become one with Christ. As a consequence of this, they were urged by the Holy Spirit to utter the word, "Abba!" ("Father!"), as *St. Paul* said (cf. Gal 4:6).

As a matter of fact, *A. Stolz* says in his book on mystical theology: "In the Eucharist there is achieved sacramentally the highest possible association with Christ in the sense of a complete transformation of our sinful being into the glorified being of Christ. Oneness with Christ frees us from our sinful being. In a sacramental mode . . . Christ lifts those who are assimilated and formed to himself out of the confines of time and conducts them before the face of the Father . . . Participation in the Eucharist gives the believer his personal rapture. Out of this world at this stage, he is led by the Son to the Father in the region of the angels, and in union with the Son he is able to stand before the Father and address him as Father."[39]

St. Therese writes, " 'My heaven' is hidden in the particle where Jesus my spouse hides himself out of love. . . . What a divine moment it is when, my dearly beloved, in your tender affection you come to transform me into you. This union of love and of unutterable bliss, 'this is my heaven'."[40]

Once more *Therese* speaks: "Jesus . . . transforms a white particle into himself every morning in order to communicate his life to you. What's more, with a love that is greater still, he wants to transform you into himself."[41]

And *St. Peter Julian Eymard:* 'This is an inexpressible union which comes next to the hypostatic union. . . . Why did Jesus Christ want to form such a union with us? To console us with his friendship, to enrich us with his graces, his merits. Above all, with the union of our lives with his and his with ours, he wanted to deify us in himself and thus fulfill the desire of the heavenly Father to crown him also in us, the members of his mystical body."[42]

The Eucharist and the Resurrection of the Body

Now we pass on to another effect which the Eucharist produces in the person who receives it under the proper conditions. We have already referred to it: the Eucharist is a cause of the resurrection of the flesh.

We are passing through times of great poverty of faith and times which are really bizarre in the substitutes they find for genuine faith. So we return to our Fathers, to great figures of all times, and to the Pope, in order to see how they interpreted or interpret now those words of Jesus which in themselves are so clear.

Irenaeus says: "Since the cup and bread become the word of God, and the Eucharist becomes the blood and the body of Christ, from which the very substance of our flesh is increased and supported, how can they [the gnostics] claim that our flesh is incapable of receiving God's gift of eternal life, when our flesh is nourished from the body and the blood of the Lord and is a member of him?"

Irenaeus continues: "Just as a cutting from the vine planted in the ground bears fruit in its season, or as a grain of wheat falling into the earth and decomposing rises . . . so also our bodies which have been nourished by the Eucharist, when they are buried in the earth and decompose, shall arise at their appointed time, because the Word of God raises them up to the glory of God the Father, who freely gives to this mortal body immortality, and to this corruptible body incorruption, because the strength of God is made perfect in weakness" (cf. 1 Cor 15:53; 2 Cor 12:9).[43]

Justin, who agrees with *Irenaeus of Lyons* and *Ignatius of Antioch* on the idea that the Eucharist is a pledge of immortality and resurrection, expresses himself, according to some commentators, "as if the Eucharist already in this life rendered our bodies immortal and had actually initiated us into the resurrection."[44]

Origen too affirms, "it communicates its own immortality (for the Word of God is immortal) to him who eats thereof."[45]

Thomas Aquinas writes, "it is proper to attribute this effect to the sacrament of the Eucharist because, as Augustine says, the word resuscitates souls but the Word made flesh enlivens bodies. It is not just the Word and his Divinity that is present in this sacrament, but the Word united to his flesh as well, and therefore it is a cause of resurrection not only for souls but also of bodies."[46]

59

In his Easter message for 1976 *Paul VI* said, "Christ the Lord is truly risen. . . . We also brethren and sons and daughters, we also will rise!. . . if with a pure and sincere heart we have fulfilled our Easter duty . . . for, of the one that is fed with this vital food, Christ has said: 'I will raise him up on the last day.' " (Jn 6:54)[47]

The Eucharist and the Transformation of the Cosmos

But the effect of the Eucharist in man goes further than that. For, as *St. Paul* says, "the whole created world eagerly awaits the revelation of the sons of God. . . . the world itself will be freed from its slavery to corruption and share in the glorious freedom of the children of God" (Rom 8:19,20). And this means that creation too is called somehow to glory.

Jesus who dies and rises again is certainly the real cause of the transformation of the cosmos. To accomplish the renewal of the cosmos, however, Jesus also expects the cooperation of people "Christified" by his Eucharist. In fact, *Paul* tells us that through our sufferings we complete "what is lacking in the sufferings of Christ" (cf. Col 1:24) and that nature "awaits the revelation of the sons of God" (Rom 8:19). One could say, therefore, that by means of the Eucharistic bread man becomes "eucharist" for the universe, in the sense that joined with Christ he is the germ of the transfiguration of the universe.

Actually, if the Eucharist is the cause of the resurrection of man, is it not possible that the body of man, divinized by the Eucharist, may be destined to decay underground in order to contribute to the renewal of the cosmos? We can say, therefore, that after we have died with Jesus we are the Eucharist for the earth. The earth eats us up as we eat the Eucharist, indeed not in order to transform us into earth but to transform the earth into "new heavens and a new earth" (Rev 21:1).

It is a fascinating thought that the bodies of our Christian dead have the task of collaborating with God in the transformation of the cosmos. This generates in our hearts deep affection and veneration for those who have preceded us. It gives us a better understanding of the age-old custom of venerating those whom we call the dead (especially saints' bodies) since they are really coming to a new life in the cosmos.

The Eucharist redeems us and makes us God. We, after dying, cooperate with Christ in the transformation of nature, so that nature turns out to be like an extension of the body of Jesus. In fact Jesus, through the incarnation, took on human nature, which is where all of nature's elements meet.

The Eucharist and Communion with our Brothers

Now let us contemplate the second chief effect of the Eucharist: that extraordinary divine fruitfulness we have talked about is produced not only in individuals; the Eucharist, as a true "sacrament of unity," also produces unity among people. And this is logical: If two persons are similar to a third, that is to Christ, they are similar to each other.

The Eucharist results in communion among brothers. And this is a glorious thing. If all mankind took it seriously, this would have unimaginable consequences. For, if we understand that the Eucharist makes us one with each other, it becomes logical to treat all men as brothers. The Eucharist forms the family of the children of God, all brothers and sisters of Jesus and of each other.

The natural family has its laws. If these were extended to a supernatural level and applied on a vast scale, they would change the world. In the family everything is shared: life itself, the house, the furniture. . . . A good family has its own intimacy: its members know one another's joys and sorrows because they communicate them. When they go out into the world they convey the warmth of their own home. They can benefit the rest of society if they reflect the integrity of a wholesome family. A family is happy when its members come together for a meal or when they sing or play together.

If the family is one of the creator's most beautiful works, what must the family of God's children be like?

In the Middle East, the common meal was given great importance. Not only did Jesus want to have his closest disciples around him at the Last Supper; but when he shared his own cup with them and broke his own bread for them, he seemed to be wanting to draw them closer to himself, almost to unite them with his own person. Jesus shows us with these external signs that the Eucharist is the sacrament of unity.

Another stupendous thing about the banquet of Jesus is that he elevated it to the level of an infinitely superior reality.

By means of the Eucharist he united Christians to himself and to each other into one single body, which is his own body. As a result, he gave the Church its most intimate and essential life: the Church is the body of

Christ, and reflects brotherhood, unity, life, and communion with God.

The Eucharist, therefore, brings about the Church, and not just part of it but the entire Church. It is the complete body of Christ present in a given place, as the letter of *Paul* makes clear: "to the Church of God which is in Corinth." (1 Cor 1:2).

The Eucharist also makes all of the members of the mystical body present, even though distances of space and separation by death may seem to divide them. Distance in space and time are nonexistent in the glorious Christ present there.

It is stated in the documents of *Vatican II,* "Celebrating the Eucharistic sacrifice, therefore, we are most closely united to the worshiping Church in heaven."[48]

In *The Acts of the Apostles,* we see how the Eucharist immediately helped Christians to become aware of being a single body: "The community of believers were of one heart and one mind. None of them ever claimed anything of his own; rather, everything was held in common" (Acts 4:32).

And *John of Damascus* writes that the Eucharist "is called *communion,* and truly is so, because of our having communion through it with Christ . . . and because through it we have communion with and are united to one another. . . . We all become one body of Christ and one blood and members of one another."[49]

Origen too says that whoever partakes of the Eucharist must become aware of what "communion with the Church" means. One of his commentators observes, "Communion with the body of Christ is communion with his bread but at the same time with his Church. The reality of the Eucharistic assembly and of each of its participants is not less important than the reality of the Eucharistic bread."[50]

Albert the Great emphasizes this reality in several passages: "As the bread, the matter of this sacrament, is made into one loaf out of many grains which share their entire makeup, compenetrating each other, so the true body of Christ is put together from many drops of blood of our own nature . . . mixed together; and thus many believers . . . united in sentiment and communicating mystically with Christ their head, constitute the body of Christ. . . . That is why this sacrament leads us to effect a communion of all our goods temporal and spiritual."[51]

The species of this sacrament, in other words, bread and wine, are symbols of communion, which means the union of many in one, because bread is prepared out of many grains and wine from many grapes."[52]

"By the very fact that Christ unites all to himself, he unites them with each other, because if several things are united to a third they are united also with each other."[53]

In conclusion, *Albert the Great* affirms, that the true body of Christ is the cause of the unity of the mystical body. The special effect of the Eucharist is the grace of incorporation, which is the supreme degree of union.[54]

The Holy Father *Paul VI* has some incomparable expressions on the Eucharist. I will quote just one: "The Eucharist . . . has been instituted to make us brothers; . . . so that from being strangers scattered far and wide and indifferent to one another, we become united, equal, and friends. It is given to change us from an apathetic and egoistic mass, from being people divided and hostile to each other, into a people, a real people, believing and loving, of one heart and of one soul."[55]

The Eucharist and the Ideal of Unity

Ours is the ideal of unity. Now, is it not significant that Jesus, in his famous prayer to the Father, should ask for unity among his disciples and among those to come, right after having instituted the Eucharist which made that unity possible?

This is how Jesus prayed while walking towards the Garden of Olives (Jn 17:11-23):

> O Father most holy,
> protect them with your name which you have
>   given me,
> that they may be one, even as we are one.

The unity between the Father and the Son is the model for our own. And we can be one as they are one because of the Eucharist.

> I do not pray for them alone.
> I pray also for those who will believe in me
>   through their word,
> that all may be one
> as you, Father, are in me and I in you;
> I pray that they may be one in us,
> that the world may believe that you sent me.

Through the Eucharist we are in Jesus, who is in the Father.

> I have given them the glory you gave me
> that they may be one, as we are one —
> I living in them, you living in me —
> that their unity may be complete.

We do not enter into the kingdom unless the unity we achieve with Jesus and with one another through the Eucharist is similar to the unity between the Father and the Son.

If we love our great ideal, our vocation to unity, we must have an immense love for the Eucharist.

The Eucharist and Man

Conditions for the Eucharist to Produce Its Full Effect.

We have considered the tremendous effects produced by the Eucharist. It is logical that they should come about in a believer if certain conditions are fulfilled.

Our incorporation into Christ, our personal deification, our complete unity with the Church, all depend on our disposition when we receive communion.

When we read the *Didache* and the early Fathers of the Church in general, we discover that the basic conditions are the following: to believe in the doctrine of Christ; to be baptized; in particular, to have faith in what the Eucharist is; to live in accordance with the teachings of Christ; to repent and to confess one's own sins in order to approach the Eucharist with a pure heart; to be reconciled with those brethren one might not be at peace with; to be in unity with the Church, with the bishop; to desire that union with Christ and with one's brothers that the Eucharist brings about.

It is written in the *Didache:* "Let no one eat or drink of the Eucharist with you except those baptized in the name of the Lord, for it was in reference to this that the Lord said: 'Do not give that which is holy to dogs.' (Mt 7:6) . . . On the Lord's Day, after you have come together, break bread and offer the Eucharist, having first confessed your offenses, so that your sacrifice may be pure. But let no one who has a quarrel with his neighbor join you until he is reconciled, lest your sacrifice be defiled."[56]

"We call this food the Eucharist," delcares *Justin,* "of which only he can partake who has acknowledged the truth of our teachings, who has been cleansed by Baptism for the remission of his sins and for his regeneration, and who regulates his life upon the principles laid down by Christ."[57]

"In the [Eucharistic] mysteries," says *John Chrysostom,* "let us not limit our attention to what falls in the range of our senses, but let us keep in mind his words. . . . The Word said, 'This is my body' (Mt 26:26). And so we must submit ourselves and believe; we must look at this with the eyes of faith. Christ has given us nothing tantible. . . . All his gifts are spiritual realities, though contained in things that are tangible. . . . For if you were incorporeal, he would have given you these incorporeal gifts without any perceptible signs; but in fact your soul is joined to your body; and so he gives you these spiritual realities in things that are tangible."[58]

Origen, commenting on this passage from *Paul:* "A man should examine himself first; only then should he eat of the bread" (I Corinthians 11:28), says that "if anyone . . . does not obey these words, but in haphazard fashion participates in the bread of the Lord and his cup, he becomes weak or sickly or, even—if I may use the expression—stunned by the power of the bread, he drops dead."[59]

And *Cyprian:* "God does not accept the sacrifice offered by one who nurses a grudge. He wants him to leave the altar and go first to be reconciled with his brother; for no one can make peace with God if he prays with hatred in his heart. The noblest sacrifice in the eyes of God is our peace, that is, harmony among brothers and a people gathered in the unity of the Father and of the Son and of the Holy Spirit."[60]

John Chrysostom says again: "Therefore let no one be a Judas. . . . If you have anything against your enemy, . . . put a stop to the hostility in order that you may be able to receive the medicine (that is, pardon) from this table. For you are approaching an awesome and holy sacrifice. Respect the meaning of this oblation. Christ lies there as the victim, and for whom and for what reason was he immolated? To join the things which belong there above to those that belong here below . . . to reconcile you with the God of the universe, to turn you from an enemy and an antagonist into a friend. . . . He did not refuse to die for you and do you refuse to pardon your own companion?. . . [This sacrifice] turns all of us into one single body since we all receive one body. Let us join therefore into one single body . . . uniting ourselves to one another with the bond of charity."[61]

Finally, *Ignatius of Antioch:* "A man who acts without the knowledge of the bishop is serving the devil."[62]

Next, we see that the great medieval theologians hand on the thought of the Fathers.

St. Albert the Great puts it like this: "Because of this charity which unites God with man and man with God, this sacrament is called the sacrament of unity and of charity. Therefore we must eat this supper in the charity of ecclesiastical unity."[63]

Thomas Aquinas says, "In a false person the sacrament does not produce any effect. We are false when the inmost self does not correspond to what is expressed externally. The sacrament of the Eucharist is an external sign that Christ is incorporated into the one who receives him and he into Christ. One is false if in his heart he does not desire this union and does not even try to remove every obstacle to it; Christ therefore does not remain in him, neither does he in Christ."[64]

Making a kind of summary of the necessary spiritual dispositions, *Paul VI* says, "In the realm of the Eucharist he understands who believes and loves. Love becomes a co-efficient of intelligence because its object is finally possessed. For the conquest of divine things love is more effective than every other spiritual faculty we have."[65]

And so, whoever approaches the Eucharist and wants to be in tune with this sacrament, must be firmly decided to achieve in his life that which the Eucharist signifies and achieves, namely unity.

Other Effects of the Eucharist

Having considered what conditions are needed for receiving the extraordinary graces of the Eucharist, let us now give some thought to what the Eucharist brings our souls, besides the principal effect of making us one body with Christ and our brothers.

I have mentioned the fact that the Eucharist is also regarded by the Church as "food for the journey," food for the people of God who are on a pilgrimage towards their final end, and thus it is called "viaticum." As such it endows our souls with an increase of love, with a consequent lessening of the passions, as *Thomas Aquinas* says.[66] It brings comfort in suffering and strength in battles and trials, until we arrive at sanctity and at eternal life.

It is the Eucharist which gives us "divine charity," "the light of wisdom," and "joy to our hearts and souls." "It stirs a man so much that it makes him go out of himself and reach the point of no longer seeing himself for himself, but himself for God, and God for God, and one's neighbor for God." These are the expressions of *Catherine of Siena.*[67]

74

And for *St. Paul of the Cross* the Eucharist is "that food of the angels which redounds also to the strengthening of the body."[68]

The Eucharist in the Life of the Christian

Of course, Eucharistic communion is not an end in itself. "The union with Christ to which this sacrament is directed . . . has to be prolonged throughout the entire life of a Christian. . . ."[69]

There is one reality of the Church that meets for the celebration of the Eucharist and manifests the *Ekklesia*. But there is another reality of the Church that is spread all over the world as a manifestation of Christ among men, as a sign of his presence.

The world does not receive the proclamation of Christ from the Eucharist so much as through the life of Christians nourished on the Eucharist and on the Word. Preaching the gospel with their lives and with their voices, they render Christ present in the midst of men.[70]

If it is united to Jesus in the Eucharist, the Christian community can and must do what Jesus has done: give its life for the world.

The life of the Church, thanks to the Eucharist, becomes the life of Jesus, a life capable of giving love, the life of God, to others, and capable of saving, since it is the very life of Jesus that is carried over to the community and to every single member in it. In this sense, we can understand the words of Paul: "And you put me back in labor pains until Christ is formed in you" (Gal 4:19).

Paul VI says that the Lord "sought to join his divine life to ours in such an intimate and loving way as to give himself to us as our nourishment and thus make us share in a personal way in his redemptive sacrifice . . . [in order] that each one of us should be inserted into and carried along in his design of salvation — which is open to all of mankind. . . ."[71]

The great theologian *Emile Mersch* explains: "The act by which Christ likens us to himself in the Eucharist is his sacrifice. The Eucharist has the tendency to make the lives of Christians a sacrifice, so that the Cross may take possession of mankind. Christ offered full reparation for sin. The faithful also offer reparation, both for themselves as individuals and on behalf of the whole mystical body; theirs is a reparation proper to members, for it continues Christ's reparation, on which it depends and from which it derives."

"Christ, the Redeemer," *Mersch* continues, "who assimilates Christians to Himself, is Christ in the greatest act of his love. His love impels him to perfect obedience to the Father and to the offering of himself as a holocaust for men [in his abandonment, we would say]. This love permeates Christians and transforms them into itself. . . . We honor [the Eucharist] more by devotedness to our fellow men than by ornate ceremonies, although the latter are also necessary."[72]

Furthermore, since modern theology has placed less emphasis on the presence of Jesus in the Eucharist, which the faithful are aware of already, than on spiritual union with him and with every member of his mystical body, Eucharistic spirituality too is directed today not so much towards the adoration of the present Lord as toward communion with him and with our brothers in every moment of the day.

The Experience of the Movement

But let's pause a moment. As we were reading these passages regarding the disposition we need for approaching the Eucharist and the effects that it produces, didn't you hear the Holy Spirit whispering in your hearts or, even more, didn't you feel like shouting out: "But this is our ideal! This is our ideal!" I confess that when I read all this I was astonished.

Do you remember, ever since we were first starting out, how carefully we prepared ourselves every morning for communion, making sure that the unity among us was perfect, and how we were ready to do without our communion if we did not pass the test of unity?

Do you remember how every morning we felt as if the Holy Spirit were knocking on the door of our spirits tirelessly repeating, "If you recall that your brother has anything against you, leave your gift at the altar, go first to be reconciled with your brother" (Mt 5:23-24)?

Do you remember our regular confessions and general confesssions in order to give a better start to our new life?

And the faith we had in the Church that would permit no doubts?

And how like a banner headline above every other was the phrase, "He who hears you, hears me" (Lk 10:16), for in our bishop we saw Christ whom we must obey?

Remember how deeply rooted in us was the conviction that no penance, no sacrifice was greater than that of loving one another as Jesus has loved us, as *Cyprian* says.[73]

And there is really no need to add what *Paul VI* has affirmed, that love was our strength during our entire lives.[74]

As for the effects, do you remember how from the first, as our love was growing, the temptations that had tormented people for their entire lives, disappeared suddenly as if by magic; then after months or years the same temptations would reappear as trials from the Lord or as a result of a slackening of their love?

And how much comfort Jesus in the Eucharist brought us during our trials when no one would give us an audience because the Movement was being evaluated by the Church. He was always there, at every hour of the day, waiting for us, telling us: after all, in the end, I am the one who is the head of the Church.

Both in our battles and in every sort of suffering, who gave us strength? We thought that we would have died many times if Jesus in the Eucharist and Jesus in our midst, nourished by the Eucharist, had not sustained us.

And the wisdom which the Movement has so much of. And the smile that characterizes its members. And the heart so often on fire. And our living for God at all times, and our knowing and telling each other that we were the luckiest people in the world. Where does all this come from? Jesus in the Eucharist!

It was he who made our whole life a continuous "spiritual exercise" — twenty-four hours a day we would never feel "down," and would always be quick to begin again if we had stopped.

Do you remember how, from the very beginning, after we met together for Mass, we would go out into all kinds of places — farms, schools, offices, and so on — to carry the news of Christ, of his new commandment, and of his gospel? We did not just repeat the doctrine but told the experience of our new life.

And our program was not a limited one. It has always been focused on the phrase "that all may be one" (Jn 17:21). Our aim was the human race, knowing that to gain its salvation, we, like Jesus, had to pay with our lives first, and talk afterwards.

That we had to offer our lives was obvious. And whenever we were asked, we offered them for the same motive: for the Church, "that all may be one."

This life has been going on for more than thirty years in our Movement; and during these days of meditating on the Eucharist, I often asked myself: but has the Eucharist always been the "motor" behind our whole life?

There is certainly a wonderful interconnection between the Eucharist and the ideal of unity. The fact that the Lord, to get this vast movement started, made us concentrate on the prayer of Jesus, on his last testament, means that he had to give us a strong push towards the only one who could accomplish it: Jesus in the Eucharist.

From the very beginning of the Movement, we noted this phenomenon just as newborn babes instinctively feed at their mothers' breasts without knowing what they are doing, so those who got to know us began to go to communion every day.

How can we explain it? What instinct is for the newborn baby, the Holy Spirit is for an adult who has been born anew into the new life that the gospel of unity brings. He is carried into the heart of Mother Church, where he feeds on the most precious nectar she has. Just look at the consequences.

Yes, this is our ideal, what in essence we have always been living, because our ideal is nothing but Christianity lived from the viewpoint of unity, the ideal of Christ.

The Eucharist and Human Society

And now I would not want to leave out another magnificent effect of the Eucharist, which *Paul VI* has sketched for us. "This communion of supernatural life," Paul says, "can have an enormous and immensely beneficial impact on every aspect of life in society. You know how this basic problem of man's social dimension towers above and dominates all others . . . how to build the earthly city. All of us know how men get caught up in this work of construction, and quite often, in fact, they manage to make remarkable progress. . . . And yet at every step they encounter obstacles and resistance within themselves simply because they lack any single transcendent principle to unify the human fabric."

"The earthly city has no reserves of faith and of love and it cannot find them in itself and of itself. But the religious city, the Church, existing within the earthly city, can supply those reserves through the tacit osmosis of example and spiritual virtue."[75]

82

"Isn't this perhaps the reason why the Eucharist is a sign to which our modern world should look with absolute trust? For it is constantly seeking and producing unity, then shattering and fragmenting it again, but always, almost in spite of itself, craving and reestablishing it; for unity, we declare, is the summit of its aspiration."[76]

The Eucharist and the Holy Spirit

And now, at the conclusion of these brief reflections on the Eucharist, I want to say a few more words about the Holy Spirit.

In his magnificent passage on the bread of life, John quotes Jesus as saying: "It is the spirit that gives life; the flesh is useless" (Jn 6:63). In this phrase Jesus refers to the role of the Holy Spirit in the Eucharistic mystery. The Holy Spirit is the principal agent every time Christ comes among us.[77] Through him the Word became flesh in Mary's womb, and it is through him that the Word becomes flesh in the host and becomes blood in the wine at the consecration of the Eucharist in every Mass.

Cyril of Jerusalem writes: "Next, after sanctifying ourselves by these spiritual songs, we ask God in his mercy to send his Holy Spirit upon our offering to make our bread the Body of Christ and our wine the Blood of Christ. For whatever the Holy Spirit touches is totally sanctified and transformed."[78]

Thus, the Mass proves to be a perpetuation of the incarnation. Surely, that is something worthy of our amazement and of our worship. The theologian Betz writes that the second-century thinkers adopt the mind of John, who "sees in the Eucharistic incarnation a sacramental continuation of Jesus' mission in the flesh."[79]

The flesh, therefore, on which we are nourished is a glorified flesh, the same flesh that Jesus possesses where he sits at the right hand of the Father. From this glorified flesh, which gives divine life, there is an out-flowing of the Holy Spirit, who forms Christ in us because we have been fed with the Eucharist.

It is the Holy Spirit, therefore, who sanctifies us for eternal life. It is through the Holy Spirit that Jesus rises in glory after his death. It is he who comes down to build the Church, the body of Christ. Again, it is the Holy Spirit who brings about unity in the community and sanctifies the community. The Holy Spirit is God, frequently silent yet continually at work, as powerfully active as he is little known; he is the Love that high-lights the Father and the Son.

As I have already indicated, God's plan for the total Christ is a magnificent journey from the Trinity back to the Trinity.

The Father loves us and sends the Son; and among the things which the Son must accomplish in conjunction with the Father, is the Eucharist. If the Son is a gift from the Father to man, the Eucharist is a gift from that first Gift. Now, when a person well disposed receives the Eucharist, being made one body with the Son and with his brothers, that person re-enters the bosom of the Father.

Here is what *Vatican II* says: "In this celebration the faithful, united with their bishop and endowed with an outpouring of the Holy Spirit, gain access to God the Father through the Son . . . they enter into communion with the most Holy Trinity."[80]

We know that there have been saints and other persons whom God has given a special task in the Church and to whom God reveals, in a more or less profound way, their immanence in the bosom of the Father.

Now generally it is not like this, not for everyone. Instead, it is being in the bosom of the Father and, at the same time, feeling a continuous longing to arrive there.

The Eucharist is food which refreshes, reinforces, and strengthens more and more, and we have to eat of it often to be able to say, "the life I live now is not my own; Christ is living in me" (Gal 2:20).

Jesus, when I set out to say something about you in the Eucharist, I think that my heart was almost on fire in my breast. I suddenly realized what I was about to do: to say something about you in four meager conversations. If I could have accomplished what I really desired, I would have built you a cathedral.

Now I feel the end result is nothing more, perhaps, than a little wooden altar. I am not capable of speaking of you. You are too great.

(I read once that if the Church did not have the Eucharist, it would not have the strength to rise up towards God, so that the Eucharist is considered to be the heart of the Church.)

And so, forgive my daring. But since your trick is to draw great things out of weakness, I offer you these pages as a tiny gift of love for your infinite gift of love. Use them so that others may know you a little better and understand how, with the strength they receive from you, they can unleash a Christian revolution in the world.

NOTES

[1] Therese of Lisieux, *Manuscrits autobiographiques,* manuscrit "B" *deuxième partie* (Lisieux, 1957), p. 236. Cf. Ronald Knox, trans., *Autobiography of St. Therese of Lisieux* (New York, 1958), p. 241.

[2] Pierre Julien Eymard, *La Sainte Eucharistie, La Présence Réelle,* Tome I (Paris, 1949), p. 87.

[3] Cf. *In Off. Festiv. Corp. Christi,* Lectio VI.

[4] Pierre Julien Eymard, p. 142.

[5] Ignatius of Antioch, *Ephesians* 19, 1 (PG 5, 660); *Ancient Christian Writers,* Vol. 1 (Westminster, Maryland, 1946), p. 67.

[6] "Decree on the Ministry and Life of Priests," 5; *The Documents of Vatican II,* ed., Walter M. Abbott, S.J. (New York, 1966), p. 541.

[7] J. Castellano, "Eucaristia" in *DES I* (Rome, 1975), p. 737.

[8] *Insegnamenti di Paolo VI,* Vol. IV (Vatican, 1967), p. 164.

[9] Pierre Benoit, cited in Castellano, p. 738.

[10] Athanasius, *Ep. fest.* 4, 3-5 (PG 26, 1377-9).

[11] Albert the Great, *De Euch.,* d. 1, c. 2, n. 7 (Borgnet edition, Vol. 38, p. 200).

[12] John Chrysostom, *In I Cor.,* hom. 24, 2 (*PG* 61, 200); cf. *The Nicene and Post-Nicene Fathers,* 1st Series, Vol. XII (Grand Rapids, 1956), p. 140.

[13] Justin, *First Apology* 1, 67, 65 (*PG* 6, 429-432, 427). *The Fathers* of the Church, Vol. 6 (New York, 1948), pp. 106-7, 105.

[14] Justin, 1, 66 (*PG* 6, 427). Translation pp. 105 f.

[15] Justin, 1, 67 (*PG* 6, 429-432). Translation p. 107.

[16] *Didache* 9, 4. *The Fathers of the Church,* Vol. 1 (New York, 1947), p. 179.

[17] Ignatius of Antioch, *Smyrnaeans 8,* 1, (PG 5, 713 f.) *The Fathers of the Church,* Vol. 1, p. 121.

[18] *The Martyrdom of St. Polycarp,* chap. 14. *The Fathers of the Church,* Vol. 1, p. 158.

[19] Irenaeus, *Adv. haer.* IV, 18, 5 (*PG* 7, 1027), in *The Ante-Nicene Fathers,* Vol. 1 (New York, 1903: American reprint of the Edinburgh edition), p. 486.

[20] For this section and the two following ones, cf. Castellano, pp. 741-745.

[21] *The Order of Mass,* U. S. Catholic Conference (Washington, D. C. , 1969), pp. 88-90.

[22] Paul VI, *Mysterium Fidei* (Encyclical *On Eucharist Doctrine and Worship),* no. 45 (Glen Rock, New Jersey, 1966), p. 44; cf. Council of Trent, *Decree On the Eucharist, chap. 1.*

[23] *Mysterium Fidei,* no. 27; cf. Council of Trent, *Doctrine de SS. Missae Sacrificio,* chap. 1.

[24] "Constitution on the Sacred Liturgy," 47-48; *The Documents of Vatican II,* p. 154.

[25] *Messale della Domenica* (Rome, 1973), pp. 441-442.

[26] Thomas Aquinas, *Summa theologiae* III, q. 79, a. 1.

[27] Thomas Aquinas, *Commentary on the Gospel of John* 6:54, 1. VII, 958.

[28] Thomas Aquinas, *Comm. in I Cor.,* c. II, 1. 5.

[29] Cf. Y. Congar - P. Rossano, "Proprietà essentiali della Chiesa," *Myst. sal.,* VII (Brescia, 1972), pp. 469-471.

[30] Cf. *The Documents of Vatican* II, p. 50, citing Leo the Great, *Serm.* 63, 7 (PL 54, 357).

[31] Thomas Aquinas, *In Sent.* IV, D. 12, q. 2, a. 1.

90

32 Cyril of Jerusalem, *Cat. myst.*, 4, 3 (*PG* 33, 1100); cf. *The Fathers of the Church,* Vol. 64 (Wash., D. C. , 1970), pp. 181-2.

33 Leo the Great, *Serm.* 63, 7 (*PL* 32, 357).

34 Augustine, *Confessions* VII, 10 (*PL* 32, 742); F. J. Sheed trans. (New York, 1943), p. 145.

35 Albert the Great, *De Euch.,* D. 3, tr. 1, c. 5 (Borgnet edition, Vol. 38, p. 257).

36 Albert the Great, *In IV Sent.* D. 9, a. 2 (Borgnet 29, 217),

37 Albert the Great, *De Euch.,* D. 3, tr. 1, c. 8, n. 2 (Borgnet 38, 272).

38 Therese of Lisieux, *Manuscrits autobiographiques,* manuscrit "A," p. 83; cf. Knox trans., p. 106.

39 A. Stolz, *Theologie der Mystik* (Regensburg, 1936), pp. 240-1.

40 Carmel de Lisieux, "Mon ciel à moi" dans *Poésies de Sainte Thérèse de l'Enfant-Jésus,* Office central de Lisieux, Lisieux, 1951, p. 31.

41 Carmel de Lisieux, "Le petit mendiant de Noël" dans *Poésie de Sainte Thérèse de l'Enfant-Jésus,* Office central de Lisieux (Lisieux 1951), p. 105.

42 Pierre Julien Eymard, *La sainte Eucharistie, La présence réelle, Tome I* (Paris 1949), p. 303-305.

43 Irenaeus, *Adv. haer.* V, 2, 3 (*PG* 7, 1124); cf. *The Ante-Nicene Fathers,* Vol. 1, p. 528.

44 D. van den Eynde, "L'Eucaristia in S. Ignazio, S. Giustino e S. Ireneo," in *Eucaristia* a cura di A. Piolanti (Rome 1957), p. 120.

45 Origen, *De orat.,* 27, 9 (*GCS* II, 365, 22-24). *Origen's Treatise on Prayer,* trans. Eric George Jay (London, 1954), p. 120.

[46] Thomas Aquinas, *Commentary on the Gospel of John* 6:55, lect. VII, 973.

[47] *Osservatore Romano,* English Edition, April 22, 1976, p. 1.

[48] "Dogmatic Constitution on the Church," 50; *The Documents of Vatican II,* p. 83.

[49] John of Damascus, *De fide orthodoxa* IV, 13 (*PG* 94, 1154). *The Fathers of the Church,* Vol. 37, p. 361.

[50] P. Jacquimont, "Origen," in *L'Eucharistie chez les premiers chrétiens* (Paris, 1976), p. 181.

[51] Albert the Great, *In Jo.* 6, 64 (Borgnet 24, 288).

[52] Albert the Great, *De eccl. hierarchia* 3, 2 (Borgnet 14, 561).

[53] Albert the Great, *In IV Sent.,* D. 8, a. 11 (Borgnet 29, 206).

[54] Albert the Great, *De euch.,* D. 3, t. 2, c. 5, n. 5 (Borgnet 38, 300).

[55] *Insegnamenti di Paolo VI,* Vol. III (1966), p. 358.

[56] *Didache* 9, 5; 14, 1-2. *The Fathers of the Church,* Vol. 1, pp. 179-182.

[57] Justin, *First Apology* 66 (*PG* 6, 427). *The Fathers of the Church,* Vol. 6, p. 105.

[58] John Chrysostom, *In Matth.,* hom. 82, 4 (*PG* 58, 743 f.). *Nicene and Post-Nicene Fathers,* first series, Vol. X, p. 495.

[59] Origen, *In Matth. comm.,* 10, 25 (*PG* 13, 904). *The Ante-Nicene Fathers,* Original Supplement to the American Edition, Vol. X (New York, 1925), p. 431.

[60] Cyprian, *De oratione dominica,* 23 (*PL* 4, 535). *The Fathers of the Church,* Vol. 36 (New York, 1958), p. 148.

[61] John Chyrysostom, *De prod. Judae,* 1, 6 (*PG* 49, 380-382).

[62] Ignatius of Antioch, *Smyrnaeans* 9, 1 (*PG* 5, 713 f.). *The Fathers of the Church,* Vol. 1. p. 122.

[63] Albert the Great, *De Euch.,* D. 3, t. 4, c. 3 (Borgnet 38, 325).

[64] Thomas Aquinas, *Commentary on the Gospel of John* 6:57.

[65] *Insegnamenti di Paolo VI,* Vol. IV (1967), p. 288.

[66] Cf. *Summa theologiae* III, q. 79, a. 6, ad 3.

[67] Catherine of Siena, as cited in *Il Messaggio di Santa Caterina da Siena* (Rome, 1970), pp. 646-648.

[68] Paul of the Cross, *Scritti spirituali* (Rome, 1974), p. 39.

[69] Sacred Congregation of Rites, *Decree on the Eucharistic Mystery,* no. 38; *The Pope Speaks,* XII (1967), 228.

[70] Cf. Castellano, p. 750.

[71] *The Pope Speaks* XIII (1968), 237.

[72] E. Mersch, *The Theology of the Mystical Body,* trans. Cyril Vollert, S.J. (St. Louis and London, 1958), pp. 592-3.

[73] Cf. Cyprian, *De oratione dominica,* 23 (*PL* 4, 535). *The Fathers of the Church,* Vol. 36, p. 148.

[74] Cf. *Insegnamenti di Paolo VI,* Vol. IV (1967), p. 288.

[75] *Insegnamenti di Paolo VI,* Vol. III (1966), pp. 355-9.

[76] *Insegnamenti di Paolo VI,* Vol. VI (1969), pp. 248-9.

[77] F. X. Durwell, *L'Eucharistie, présence du Christ* (Paris, 1971), pp. 45-7.

[78] Cyril of Jerusalem, *Cat. myst.,* 5, 7 (*PG* 33, 1113). *The Fathers of the Church,* Vol. 64, p. 196.

[79] J. Betz in *Myst. Sal.,* VII (Brescia), pp. 261-2.

[80] "Decree on Ecumenism," 15; *The Documents of Vatican II,* p. 358.